Original title:
Whispers Beneath the Ice

Copyright © 2024 Creative Arts Management OÜ
All rights reserved.

Author: Riley Donovan
ISBN HARDBACK: 978-9916-94-490-5
ISBN PAPERBACK: 978-9916-94-491-2

The Soundless Lull of Winter's Embrace

Frosty toes and chilly noses,
Snowmen grinning like silly poses,
Slipping here and tripping there,
Winter giggles fill the air.

Hot cocoa spills, a marshmallow dive,
Sledding down hills, oh what a drive!
Tumbling down with puffs of white,
Laughing hard in pure delight.

Icicles hang like frozen fangs,
Players roll in winter's tangs,
Snowball flights through frosty lanes,
Yet all we hear are giggles and gains.

Snowflakes dance like jolly sprites,
Frosty breath in frosty bites,
We'll thaw our hearts with joyous cheer,
For winter fun is always near.

Beneath the Shroud of Snow

Snowflakes dance like tiny clowns,
As snowmen wear their frosty crowns.
A squirrel slips on icy ground,
His acorn lost, it won't be found.

With every step, a crunching sound,
The cold air makes our voices bound.
We share a laugh, a frosty cheer,
In winter's realm, we lose our fear.

Voices Lost in Arctic Dreams

In dreams, polar bears wear hats,
They sip hot cocoa, chat with bats.
A penguin jives in snowball fights,
While seals are joking, oh what sights!

The frost invites our silly schemes,
As laughter echoes through our dreams.
We play tag with the drifting flake,
A frozen world, just for fun's sake.

The Quiet Pulse of the Glacial Heart

The glacier beats a frosty drum,
While penguins prance, they're never glum.
In icy caves, the snowmen giggle,
As snowballs fly, the kids just wriggle.

A polar fox starts doing tricks,
As everyone cracks jokes and quick quips.
The frozen air, a stage so bright,
For playful hearts in winter's light.

Enigmatic Chills of Forgotten Tales

Old tales of snow have gone awry,
With yeti myths that make us cry.
A snowflake prince, he lost his shoe,
And snowball fights, a royal view.

In icy forests, secrets hide,
As snowmen plot with mistletoe tied.
With frozen laughs and jolly cheer,
The chilly air brings warmth right here.

Beneath the Stillness

In the chill where snowflakes play,
Penguins slide in a comical way.
A walrus bumbles, tries to dance,
As seals giggle in a frosty trance.

Icebergs wobble, tipping like fools,
While fish wear their best party jewels.
The frost whispers secrets, oh so sly,
As snowmen laugh and snowballs fly.

Voices Stir

Amidst the ice, a squirrel grins,
In a frozen gauntlet of furry wins.
A bear in shades sips icy tea,
While fish dive down for a spree.

The frosty pals crack a frigid joke,
A penguin slips, the crowd goes broke.
Snowflakes dance in a swirling maze,
As the sun peeks out, they bask in rays!

Subdued Symphony of the Glacial World

A jazzy tune plays on the frost,
That polar bears can't help but gloss.
They tap their paws, keepin' the beat,
As penguins join in, all light on their feet.

Icicles chime, oh what a sound!
Each note a giggle, joy all around.
Nutty snowmen start a grand song,
While bouncy snowballs come rolling along.

In the Grip of the Frozen Silence

Under layers thick, where laughter sneaks,
A fridge of jokes, without any squeaks.
A snowball fight breaks the icy peace,
As cold critters throw with great caprice.

Chilly giggles fill the bright air,
With frosted faces, the fun's quite rare.
A moose in a hat tells all a tale,
As winter's humor begins to prevail.

The Hidden Chorus of the Chilled Depths

In the depths where frosty critters play,
A symphony of chuckles takes the day.
The ice creaks as a seal takes a dive,
While otters spin, oh how they thrive!

Beneath blankets of snow, secrets unfold,
With penguins trading stories bold.
Each laugh, a bubble in the frozen sea,
While warmth sparkles, bright and free!

Resounding Solitude of the Ice World

In a world where penguins play,
They slide and slip in a jolly way.
Snowflakes giggle as they drift,
While polar bears look for a gift.

Frosty air holds a frosty joke,
As seals pop up, and then they soak.
A game of tag, they all partake,
In chilly fun, they never break.

Icicles hang like pointy teeth,
As snowmen dance with merry glee.
The ice cap sings a glacial tune,
While turtles twirl 'neath the bright moon.

Amongst the drifts, a snowball flies,
Friendly battles 'neath azure skies.
Laughter echoes, crisp and bright,
In this frosted world, pure delight.

Beneath Layers of Crystal Stillness

Beneath the sheen of icy sheets,
A critter's gathering of frozen treats.
Blizzards chortle, the snowmen smile,
While snowflakes twirl, each with their style.

Skiing squirrels zip through the trees,
Cheeky penguins chill, if you please.
Frosty giggles in the air,
As they skate with grace, without a care.

Icicles dangle like funny hats,
While snowball fights erupt with spats.
The ice laughs softly, a frozen jest,
In this snowy realm, they feel so blessed.

Under the frost, a party brews,
With chilly drinks and frosty views.
The cold wraps them in a cozy hug,
Creating smiles, a snowy shrug.

Silent Murmurs of the Frozen Depths

In icy caves where secrets sleep,
The bear takes naps while penguins leap.
Each flake of snow a whispered joke,
As laughter bubbles from thawed oak.

Snowmen argue about their hats,
While clever foxes chase their gnats.
The frozen river plays a prank,
As fish jump up from their chilly bank.

Frosty winds weave tales so sly,
As frosty owls croon lullabies.
With each crack of ice, a giggle grows,
In this realm where chilly humor flows.

Glacial paths pave a world of play,
Where snowflakes dance in a gleeful sway.
With each step taken on crystal floors,
The spirit of fun forever soars.

Secrets Entombed in Crystal Silence

Beneath silence thrives a hidden laugh,
As snowflakes spin in a fluid path.
A troupe of seals throws a wild ball,
While yetis groove at a waltzing hall.

Frozen streams echo soft, sweet quips,
As penguins practice their funny flips.
Each shimmer holds a chuckle sly,
In the frosty sphere where spirits fly.

Snowy mounds hide a secret dance,
Where critters leap in a frosty trance.
The chill may bite, but joy stays warm,
In this cool haven, free from harm.

Under the frost, they party and cheer,
With frosty beer that will never smear.
The world above might freeze and frost,
But in this heart, no giggle's lost.

Hushed Tales of the Icy Abyss

In frozen realms where penguins dance,
They slip and slide, not taking a chance.
A walrus snorts, trying to sing,
While seals clap paws, doing their thing.

An icefish jokes in scales so bright,
'This chill is great, but where's the light?'
With frosty breath, they share their glee,
In laughter's grip, so wild and free.

Shivers of Solitude in the Cold

A polar bear dons shades of flair,
Sipping on cocoa, without a care.
'I lost my hat!' a snowman sighs,
As icicles melt, revealing their lies.

An ardent owl with feathers that cluck,
Wonders aloud, 'Is it just bad luck?'
The frosty breeze, a soft lament,
While penguins joke from their mobile tent.

Echoing Songs from the Below

Beneath the surface, where bubbles rise,
A fish hums tunes that pleases the eyes.
'Is that a whale I hear?' one clam asks,
While sea cucumbers don quirky masks.

The krill all giggle, in tiny masses,
Sharing their tales of blizzard classes.
With icy beats and laughter outpoured,
They revel in merriment, unbored.

The Stillness that Speaks

In silence profound, a snowflake lands,
Tickling the toes of Arctic bands.
A fox sneezes, 'Ain't that just grand?'
While rabbits plot a snowball stand.

An old igloo whispers secrets untold,
'Time for ice cream that never gets cold!'
With chuckles echoing through frosty space,
They sip warm soup with snow in their face.

Beneath the Shrouded Ice

In the frosty depths, there's a riddle,
Penguins in tuxedos playing the fiddle.
They dance on the ice, without a care,
While seals on the sidelines just stop and stare.

A snowman tries to join in the fun,
But his carrot nose... came undone!
As he rolls and tumbles, he makes quite a sound,
The winter is laughing, joy abounds!

Silence of Eternal Winter

The snowflakes giggle as they drift down,
Twirling and spinning, oh what a clown!
Polar bears slip in their fuzzy boots,
Chasing after snowballs like hairless scoots.

Frosty the snowman, he tells a tall tale,
Of a penguin who tried to sail a gale.
He ended up surfing on a big ice floe,
And the fish in the sea said, 'Whoa, did you see that show?'

Ghostly Murmurs in Frigid Waters

Under the surface, fish start to plot,
They're planning a party, quite a hot shot!
Dressed in kelp, they're ready to vibe,
A disco ball made from a crab's old tribe.

The mermaids giggle, doing the twist,
While the seaweed sways, they just can't resist.
They laugh as the tides play hopscotch with the moon,
In a frozen realm, where each note's a boon!

Subterranean Secrets of the Blizzards

In caverns below, a mystery brews,
Rabbits wearing helmets, plotting their views.
They're building an empire of carrots and snow,
While giraffes say, 'Can we come on the show?'

Yet lost in their dreams, polar foxes convene,
Creating hot cocoa that's fit for a queen.
They invite all the critters for a toast and a cheer,
'Cause wintertime giggles are the best time of year!'

Soliloquies of the Shimmering Cold

In a world that's chillier than an unbrushed tooth,
Penguins debate what's a good age for swooth.
Snowflakes giggle as they flutter down,
Wearing tiny hats that make them look quite clown.

Icicles dangle like toothpicks on high,
They poke at the clouds, asking them why.
Frosty tongues wag, trading jokes from the past,
While winter's cold breath makes all good times last.

Beneath the Frozen Horizon

Polar bears ponder, 'Is this a silent retreat?'
While walruses argue about who has more feet.
Seals do ballet on their icy white stage,
Pretending the chill is all part of the rage.

The snowdrifts chuckle, piled high in a mound,
As important as taxes, they keep it profound.
A blizzard struts in, all haughty and proud,
As lowly old leaves hide, feeling quite cowed.

Echoes in the Icebound Cavern

In the caverns so frosty, an echo's a blast,
Where the echoes of laughter seem stuck to the past.
A snowman's a lawyer, with his hat set askew,
He defends all the snowballs—'That's not what I threw!'

The icicles argue about weight and their length,
While snowflakes just roll, laughing hard at their strength.

Each drip like a giggle breaks up the grand freeze,
As ice skates start dancing but slip with such ease.

Veiled Songs of the Snowy Depths

Deep in winter's grip where no one can peek,
The snow critters sing in a tune oh so cheek.
A squirrel in snow boots tells tales with a grin,
While rabbits hold contests for fluffiest skin.

The shadows play pranks, sliding under the moon,
While ice cubes are jiving, humming a tune.
A snow angel requests a more jazzy beat,
Shaking off snowflakes stuck to their feet.

The Quietude of Crystalline Depths

In the silent chill, snowmen scheme,
With carrots for noses and a frosty dream.
Penguins wobble in their tuxedo suits,
Arguing over the best fishy roots.

Underneath, the fish all laugh and jest,
Sardines hold karaoke, they're truly the best.
Icebergs roll their eyes in a frozen play,
While seals throw shells in a frosty ballet.

Timeless Echoes of Arctic Dreams

The polar bear grins with a goofy stance,
As he trips on ice, giving fish a chance.
Snowflakes giggle as they swirl and twirl,
A chilly dance in a frosty whirl.

In the depths, a lobsters' conga line,
With seaweed hats that sparkle and shine.
They boast of adventures in their frosty realm,
While an owl hoots stories from a snowy helm.

Whispers from the Glacial Light

Frosty rabbits with their fluffy tails,
Plan silly pranks and ride on whale trails.
Icicles dangle, trying to hold back,
Laughter erupts as they crack with a whack.

Tricky little otters, with their slippery ways,
Slide down the ice in a comical craze.
Snowflakes jump in to join the fun,
Who knew the cold could be number one?

Stories Encased in Frozen Echoes

A walrus tells tales of a snowball fight,
While penguins gather, all eager for spite.
They toss with glee in the wintery air,
Creating a spectacle beyond compare.

Frosty wishes on snowflakes abound,
As yetis perform to a joyful sound.
Laughter erupts from the icy expanse,
Nature's humor in a frosty dance.

Cold Secrets Entangled in Time

In a realm where snowflakes gossip,
Ice cubes chuckle, looking quite posh.
Polar bears throw snowball fights,
As penguins dance in a snowy swash.

Frosty jokes make sleds go fast,
While fish might drop their scales in glee.
A snowman wears a hat so grand,
It's a wonder he can stand with glee!

Yet under layers, secrets spin,
Like turtles twirling in frosty bliss.
With each tumble, ice socks and spins,
Caught in a frosty ice dance twist!

So let's delight in chilling tales,
Of frosty friends and icy fun.
For in this cold, laughter prevails,
As we all bask in winter sun.

Lament of the Submerged Voices

Under layers, voices riddle,
Like fish in hats on a frosty spree.
A duck quacks to a turtle's fiddle,
While seals debate who swims most free.

Icicles dangle like frozen tongues,
Sharing secrets of days gone by.
Lingering laughs on the lips of youngs,
As frost captures every sly cry.

Beneath the chill, jokes do not tire,
With laughter echoing through the depth.
Fish tales of icy, outrageous fire,
Now told by a walrus's deft heft.

So hark to the giggles and playful moans,
Frozen tales meant for silly nights.
In chilly depths where joy condones,
Fun thrives in frosty delights.

Frosted Secrets by Frigid Light

In the glow of a cold moonlight,
Ice crystals twinkle with hints of glee.
Snowflakes giggle in a playful flight,
While seals slip on ice with great esprit.

Snowmen tell knock-knock jokes at dawn,
Their carrot noses scrunching with cheer.
Under the ice, a wise old fish fawn,
Reveals secrets that we all hold dear.

With frozen chuckles, they scatter wide,
As snow slides down from a hill's tall crest.
Frosty pals gather, side by side,
In a comedy show that's quite the jest!

So here's the scoop in snowy lands,
Laughter lingers in the crisp night air.
With every slip, hilarity expands,
In their frozen world of carefree flair.

Subtle Breaths from the Hallowed Ice

Along the banks where ice meets the sway,
Grass giggles softly lest it be seen.
Frogs croak silly songs through the fray,
As they hop with glee, bright and green.

Beneath the glimmer of a crystalline show,
Secrets of ice echo soft and clear.
With quickened beats, the heart's cozy glow,
Unfolds the chilly jest without fear.

Penguins waddle in their best tuxedo,
Spinning tales of snowball picnics galore.
As they fall in heaps, knee-deep in shadow,
Laughter bounces off their chilly floor.

So let us toast to the fun we've gleaned,
In these frozen realms where joy is rife.
For the bonds of laughter stay evergreen,
As we dance through the frost, frosty life!

Chilled Soliloquies of Enduring Bondage

Oh frosty friend, you're rather blue,
Stuck here in snow, what shall we do?
The penguins dance, they think it's grand,
As you complain, stuck in this land.

A snowman's hat gets blown away,
He screams aloud, 'Please come and play!'
The chilly breeze, it gives me glee,
Your icy grip? It's home to me!

But ice can crack, oh what a fate,
A slip and slide, oh, isn't it great?
With every slip, we laugh and moan,
'This frozen world, it feels like home!'

So here we are, in winter's clutch,
With icy hugs that mean so much,
Through chills and thrills, we'll make it last,
A cool romance, a frosty blast!

Unearthed Secrets of the Winter's Heart

What secrets lie beneath this frost?
Do snowflakes know what we have lost?
They twirl and swirl, in frigid flight,
Giggling echoes of a snowy night.

I once found a rabbit, don't you see?
He winked at me, then ran for free!
I chased him down, the slippery slope,
This winter's madness fuels my hope!

A snowball fight breaks out nearby,
While icicles hang and children cry,
The chuckles rise like frosty steam,
On winter's stage, we laugh and dream.

With secret frost, we'll write our tale,
Of icy trails and one big fail,
So grab your sled, let's take a ride,
In snowy chaos, let's confide!

The Absence of Sound Beneath the Ice

It's quiet here, a frigid pause,
Do penguins giggle? They'll get applause!
As silence reigns, I start to dance,
This frozen stage, a silly chance.

Cracking ice, a subtle pop,
What was that? Oh, please don't stop!
A snowshoe hare hops in delight,
While I fumble in the quiet night.

A lone ice cube clinks, or was that me?
Chilled fools gather for a comedy spree,
Making jokes with frosty breath,
Who knew that cold could feel like warmth in death?

The air is thick with giggles unspoken,
In winter's grasp, we find a token,
So here we sit, in winter's play,
Finding joy in the frozen fray!

Shivering Sentiments from Below

A glacier's sigh, so deep and wide,
While ice skaters glide with boisterous pride,
But below the surface, it's quite a mess,
With fish in tuxedos, they truly impress!

"Did you see that?" a walrus cried,
"Fell on my flipper!" he lied with pride,
The fish just chuckled, gave a swish,
"Next time aim for a bigger wish!"

Slippery games, it's quite the show,
Frosty floors, with a shove and go,
We tumble down in a hearty heap,
And share our laughs in the frost-kissed sweep.

So beneath this layer, we find our fun,
With banter bright as the wintry sun,
Through frosty gales and icy bends,
Our shivering hearts will always be friends!

Shadows of the Frozen Depths

In frigid lands where penguins dance,
A snowman's hat gives quite a chance.
They waltz above frozen fish so sly,
While seals below just roll and sigh.

Icicles giggle, their sharp jokes told,
Chasing the drifts, they certainly bold.
A snowflake slips—oh what a sight!
Painfully landing, it says, "Not quite!"

Voices Echoed in Crystal Silence

In a cave of glitter, snowball fights break,
Echoes of laughter, oh what a mistake!
A yeti loses balance, tumbles down,
Heads turn, the whole mountain wears a frown.

Frosty frogs leap with a comical croak,
Joking with snowmen, who sips on smoke.
Chilled air tries to stifle the jokes,
Yet merry chuckles rise from the folks.

The Frost's Enigmatic Lullaby

Napping cats, in sweaters snug,
Chase after snowflakes, giving a tug.
Their tails flick while they slide and slip,
Dreaming of fish on a wintry trip.

A polar bear complains, "It's a bit too cold!"
While a squirrel nearby, grabs nuts like gold.
They swap silly stories, with twinkling eyes,
As glittering stars grin from snowy skies.

Hidden Stories in Chilled Waters

Beneath the ice, the fish meet to chat,
Trading old secrets like friends on a mat.
"Who stole my snack?" one glittered fish croaks,
As the rest giggle like a troupe of blokes.

Seal pups weigh in, with their chubby sass,
Making a fuss about lunchtime grass.
Fish start a club, with a sign that reads,
"Join us for laughter and plenty of weeds!"

Echoes of the Frigid Unknown

In a land where snowflakes dance,
Frosty creatures sing and prance.
An arctic squirrel plays a tune,
Chasing shadows 'neath the moon.

Penguins waddle with such flair,
Icebergs laugh without a care.
Frosty chuckles fill the air,
While snowmen trade their winter wear.

Polar bears with silly hats,
Swim through ice in flapping spats.
Chilly jokes and frosty puns,
Keep the cold from weighing tons.

In this freeze, the ice gets loose,
Making room for playful moose.
Beneath the chill, a giggle hides,
Tucked away where laughter bides.

Voices Lurking in the Frost

In winter's grip, the snowflakes pry,
Bubbles rise up, oh my, oh my!
A snowman sneezes, ice goes fly,
And penguins laugh, they can't deny.

The icicles hum a jolly tune,
As frosty critters congregate soon.
A polar bear does silly tricks,
While the seals all giggle and mix.

Beneath the crust, they hide and scheme,
Snowy pranks like a frosty dream.
A rabbit somersaults with glee,
Wonders what the cold will be.

Snowball fights with frosted flair,
Chilly laughter fills the air.
It's a comedy on frozen ground,
In every flake, joy can be found.

Beneath the Glacial Veil

Icebergs play peek-a-boo in style,
While seals in tuxedos pose awhile.
Fluffy snowflakes descend like confetti,
With penguins that waddle all too petty.

A hare with a scarf darts to and fro,
While snowflakes dance in a wintry show.
Grumpy walruses roll in delight,
As frosty giggles ignite the night.

Hidden jokes in the snowy drift,
An Arctic party, oh what a gift!
Beneath the freeze, a secret thrill,
Chilled laughter echoes, giving a chill.

The frost ticks jokes like a frosty clock,
Each frozen breath, a tick and a tock.
With every snowflake that twirls and twirls,
The icy jokes turn into pearls.

Chilling Secrets of the Subsurface

Under the surface, where no one peeks,
The ice holds secrets, and frosty squeaks.
Snowflakes gossip with frosty bites,
About penguins' shenanigans and ice-skating flights.

An undercurrent of laughter flows,
Where slippery seals wear winter clothes.
A chill in the air and laughter spins,
As polar bears coordinate some wins.

Under the glimmer, mischief abounds,
Blowing bubbles, the ice breaks bounds.
Snowmen dance with giddy glee,
While winter blusters, 'Come join me!'

In frosty layers, a cabin waits,
For jolly critters and ice-bound mates.
With every crack, a chuckle grows,
In this frozen world, anything goes!

Tales from the Underneath

In layers deep, the tales are spun,
Where fish play poker, just for fun.
An octopus juggles pearls with glee,
While narwhals dance, a sight to see.

A snowman sneezes, then starts to roll,
His carrot nose, a digging tool.
The clams all giggle, tucked in their beds,
As seals throw snowballs, aimed at their heads!

The icebergs chuckle, with cracks so wide,
Misfits of winter, no place to hide.
The turtles spin stories, full of flair,
While frosty fairies brush up their hair.

From the depths, a laugh echoes clear,
With frosty puns that all can hear.
It's quite a party, beneath the chill,
A comedy club, on a frosty hill.

Echoing Silence of Winter's Depth

In the frozen realm, where shadows glide,
The penguins skate, no need to hide.
A walrus tricks with a seal's big hat,
While polar bears giggle at the spat.

"Why did the ice cube get a job?" they tease,
"Because he wanted to chill with ease!"
The glaciers glimmer with laughter's might,
As snowflakes swirl, in a frosty flight.

Beneath the crust, the laughter flows,
With cheeky comments that nobody knows.
A whale plays guitar, serenades the night,
While snowshoe hares hop in sheer delight.

Through the icy caverns, a joke takes flight,
As critters gather, all dressed in white.
With a chuckle and shiver, they hold on tight,
For even the cold can bring warmth in sight.

Chilling Secrets of the Icebound Valley

Amidst the snowflakes, secrets dwell,
Where polar bears laugh at their own smell.
The bunnies giggle, with twitching ears,
As they tell tales that melt all fears.

The fish in schools, they play charades,
With icebergs giggling at their escapades.
A frigid wind hums a silly tune,
As snowflakes dance beneath the moon.

In the valley deep, the moose takes a sip,
Of hot cocoa, while the fox does a flip.
"Why did the icicle break up today?"
"Because it found someone who wouldn't sway!"

So listen closely, hear the cheer,
In the chilling valley, nestled near.
With jokes and jests, the laughter grows,
In frosty corners, where mirth bestows.

The Frost-Laden Gaze

Under the frost, a play unfolds,
With snowmen gossiping, breaking molds.
A polar bear wears socks, quite a sight,
While toppings on snow cones feel just right.

A snowflake slips, and then it blurs,
"With ice like this, it calls for slurs!"
The owls remark with their wise old eyes,
While the shivering bunnies avoid the pies.

Icicles dangle, with wonderful flair,
As winter critters begin to declare.
"Why don't we warm up with a good tale?
Of snowball fights and a speedy snail!"

So let's toast marshmallows, all around,
In this frosty realm, laughter's the sound.
With giggles and grins, they all abide,
In the icicle kingdom, where fun takes a ride.

Frozen Melodies Lost to Time

Beneath the frost, the tunes lay still,
Humming to the chill, a frozen thrill.
Snowflakes dance with a frosty twirl,
While penguins plot a silly swirl.

Icicles drip like a drip-drop beat,
Where snowmen groove with frozen feet.
When wind changes, they shake it off,
A chilly laugh, a snowy scoff.

In the gleam of the starry night,
Polar bears try to dance with fright.
Their paws slip, with a bumbling sway,
Chasing snowflakes that dance away.

In silence, secrets start to hum,
As walruses join the frozen fun.
Each chuckle coated with glistening glaze,
Lost in time, through winter's maze.

The Cold's Silent Confessions

In the frosty air, secrets reside,
Snowmen chuckle, with nothing to hide.
From frozen lips, silly stories shared,
While frosty llamas grin, slightly impaired.

An igloo party, held on a slab,
With ice cubes clinking, what a fab!
The chairs are cold, but laughter's warm,
As snowy critters strut in charm.

A seal sings off-key, a comical croon,
As blizzards join in, dancing to the tune.
Icicles swaying in the winter light,
Chase away shadows, hold the night tight.

Even the chill cannot stifle glee,
In this frozen land, wild and free.
With every laugh, spirits rise and glide,
It's the cold that keeps our joy inside.

Echoes from the Polar Depths

Bubbles pop with a playful glee,
In icy waters, life's a spree.
Selves beneath the frozen sheet,
Fish in tuxedos, oh what a treat!

Polar bears pondering pizza pies,
With toppings of snow, much to their surprise.
Their thoughts echo in the biting air,
Fluffy clouds drift without a care.

Nibbles from seals and flippers that clap,
Creating echoes in a frosty nap.
Each sound a giggle, a joyful shout,
In the chilly depths, there's no doubt.

From layers thick, behold the cheer,
Where laughter's contagious, never sincere.
Frozen tales that chill the spine,
Yet all absurd, and just so fine!

Underneath the Thawing Silence

In the thawing hush, giggles arise,
Where icebergs melt, and mischief lies.
Penguins slide in a slapstick race,
Flopping around, what a comical place!

The sun peeks in with a cheeky grin,
As snowballs fly, let the fun begin!
Each frozen chuckle resounds like bells,
Where secrets echo, and humor dwells.

A snow hare hops with a bounce so spry,
While bunnies compose their own lullaby.
The frost may bite, but hearts are light,
In a world where laughter wins the fight.

So let the warmth trickle down like rain,
As we dance 'neath the thaw, and break the chain.
In frigid air, the funny takes flight,
A frosty delight, from day to night.

Lament of the Shattered Surface

When the ice cracked, oh what a sound,
Fish were startled, flipping around.
Three penguins squealed, 'Is this the end?'
While a seal laughed, 'Let's all pretend!'

A snowman flew past, looking quite bold,
Said, 'I'm not melting, just turning gold!'
His carrot nose slipped, fell on the ground,
As everyone chuckled at the icy rebound.

A polar bear slid, lost in a shamble,
With ice cubes clattering, what a big gamble!
He waved at the penguins, who yelled with glee,
'Take a seat, dear friend, this ice is free!'

Thus, they all slid, on a frostbitten spree,
Laughing and playing, a cold jubilee.
Surface may shatter, jokes break the chill,
In the heart of winter, we find our thrill.

Dreams Entombed in Winter's Grasp

Beneath the layers, secrets do lie,
A walrus snores, dreaming of pie!
Snowflakes giggle as they land with a plop,
'We need some warmth, let's just take a shop!'

Icicles dangle, sharp as a knife,
A squirrel queries, 'Is this really life?'
Bundled in snow, he makes quite the sight,
'This winter retreat is a comical fright!'

The hare builds a fort, made of pure frost,
With marshmallow snowmen, what a kooky cost!
'Join us for cocoa!' calls out from the glen,
'Unless you prefer to nap like a hen!'

As winter chuckles, shivers in glee,
Trapped dreams come out, how goofy they be.
Laughter rings loud, under layers so deep,
In this frosty kingdom, we dance while we sleep.

Unseen Currents of the Thaw

As the sun peeks through, the ice starts to sway,
Fish in the deep plan a wild getaway.
'We're swimming to freedom, escape from this hold!'
While the otters go 'Whee!' in the water so cold!

Cracks start to form, like a joker's sly grin,
A beaver yells, 'Hold tight, here we go again!'
Rabbits skitter sideways, slipping on snow,
'Next stop, the buffet, let's put on a show!'

Drifting along, on a melty romance,
A polar bear waltzes, in a slippery dance.
All the critters cheer, 'There goes our king!'
As he tumbles over, shouting, 'I can sing!'

Thus life flows like water, across the ice crust,
Giggling and splashing, in frosty we trust.
Currents of chuckles, hidden but bright,
In spring's lacy laughter, everything's right.

Echoes of the Cold's Embrace

In this frozen realm, where laughter begins,
Chilling tales dance, like comical sins.
A bear with a scarf, all muddled in style,
Chased by arctic fox — oh, that's quite a mile!

Echoes resound, like a kite in full flight,
As snowflakes chuckle, 'Don't take it too tight!'
Snowmen do jiggles, trying to break free,
With noses so orange, they beckon with glee.

In icy caverns, gags flourish like blooms,
'Tell me your dreams, before winter consumes!'
The air's filled with mirth, and a pinch of the chill,
Every giggle sparkles, with joyous goodwill.

So here's to the frosty, the fun, and the wild,
Where even the cold can be happily styled.
Echoes of laughter in a snowy embrace,
Bring warmth to the heart, in this whimsical space.

Murmuring Spirits of the Cold

In the frost, the giggle sneaks,
Snowflakes laugh with chilly cheeks.
A penguin slips on ice so sly,
Then shakes his head as snowballs fly.

The frostbite's tickle makes them dance,
An icicle drips in a frozen prance.
The snowmen chat with carrot noses,
Freezing jokes, but nobody dozes!

A polar bear in furry disguise,
Plays hide and seek, oh what a surprise!
The ice cubes clink in a wild jest,
Sipping cold soda, they're feeling blessed.

Beneath the chill, a snowball fight,
Giggles erupt in the pale moonlight.
In the heart of winter's sporting spree,
The frosty jesters run wild and free.

Frozen Testaments of Time

In a world where icicles grin,
Old folks tell tales of snow and sin.
A snowflake fell from on high,
Landed softly, oh me, oh my!

Frosty breath and frostier puns,
Stirring up laughter, oh what fun!
Icicles like teeth, so sharp and bright,
Be careful when you take a bite!

A snowshoe hare on a sled so slick,
Races the wind, oh what a trick!
Time stands still in a crystal ball,
Who knew that winter could be such a ball?

The hourglass fills with glimmering frost,
In this chilly realm, no one's lost.
Every tick-tock held with glee,
Just frozen fun beneath the spree!

Shadows of the Frigid Whisper

Underneath the snowy night,
Ice sprites giggle, what a sight!
Their shadows dance in the pale moon,
Playing charades to winter's tune.

A pile of snow makes a comfy bed,
Two cheeky robins joke instead.
They fluff and flounder out in the cold,
Whispering secrets, bold and old.

A rabbit giggles as he hops,
Making snow angels, never stops.
Winter's laughter fills the air,
Chattering creatures without a care.

Each flake is a joker, each drift a laugh,
Winter's stage, the craziest half.
Yet in the stillness, fun holds sway,
As shadows frolic on icy ballet.

Eulogies of the Waiting Sea

The ocean sighs beneath a sheet,
Waiting for thaw in a dance so neat.
Crabs in winter boots tap their toes,
Reciting tales of flurries and woes.

With frozen echoes, the waves hum light,
Telling secrets of the starlit night.
A fishy joke that drifts like a dream,
Icy gales join in, a whimsical scheme.

Seagulls wearing scarves swoop and glide,
As frosty currents frolic and slide.
In this coastal chill where laughter's free,
The icebound tales flow through the sea.

As the tide waits for warmer cheer,
It's all just fun, my friends, no fear.
In the pauses, laughter breaks through,
The cold's a comedian, you'll see it too!

Frostbitten Whispers of Forgotten Times

In a land where frostflakes giggle,
Snowflakes dance and then they wiggle.
An old penguin tells a joke so bright,
The seal starts laughing with all its might.

Icicles laugh as they hang around,
With each drip, they make merry sound.
A polar bear trips on a slippery spot,
And the walruses chuckle, loving the plot.

The snowmen argue about their hats,
While the arctic fox chats with the chitchat cats.
The winter sun grins, oh what a sight,
As the blizzards swirl with pure delight.

So here in the cold, where the giggles roam,
Frostbitten tales feel just like home.
With each silly laugh and frigid cheer,
Winter's humor brings us all near.

The Unseen Stories in Ice

Beneath the surface, a joke is told,
Frozen fish chuckle, their humor bold.
A curious crab plays peek-a-boo,
With a dancing snowflake that's winking too.

A bear's got a hat made of frozen fluff,
He struts like a king, thinking he's tough.
But a gust of wind sends him for a spin,
And suddenly all the critters join in.

Icebergs giggle like bubbles of tea,
As they break apart with sheer glee.
A snowball fight erupts on the shore,
With giggles and laughter, who could ask for more?

So lend an ear, let fun take flight,
In a world where cold brings humor bright.
For beneath the chill, fun stories freeze,
Ready to thaw with the funniest tease.

Songs of the Subzero Shadows

In shadows cast by a blizzard's breath,
A choir of critters sings of warmth and depth.
A seal with a scarf hits all the right notes,
While the polar bear conducts with antics and quotes.

A walrus winks, sporting a cool mustache,
Playing the drums made of frozen trash.
Each crack of ice is a beat in the song,
As the skaters slip and glide along.

Squirrels in mittens come out to parade,
Beneath the frost, their antics don't fade.
They roll in the snow, and tumble with glee,
Singing nonsense tunes, just wild and free.

Oh, sing loud, dear friends, beneath the cold sky,
For laughter is winter's sweetest reply.
In subzero shadows, our voices collide,
Creating a symphony where joy can't hide.

Beneath the Slumbering Surface

Under the crust, where cold dreams dwell,
A sleepy bear dreams of sausages, oh so swell.
With tiny fish and seals who conspire,
To craft a picnic atop frozen mire.

Snowflakes sprinkle their giggles like dust,
As snowmen stand guard, it's a must!
With carrot noses twitching in jest,
They plan a snowball fight, a wintery quest.

Icicles dangle, acting all tough,
But melt with laughter when told they're not buff.
A wise old owl, perched, gives a hoot,
While the nearby rabbits munch on sweet root.

So peek beneath, where the fun is alive,
In a world of frost, the jokes will thrive.
With each frosty chuckle and frolic that's free,
Winter's mischief is a sight to see.

Sibilant Shadows Beneath the Snow

Frosty friends in a frozen dance,
Giggles echo at every chance.
Socks made of snow, toes feeling neat,
With snowman hats, oh what a treat!

Snowflakes tumble like giggling sprites,
Chasing each other on frosty nights.
A snowball fight, with laughter loud,
We roll in flakes, feeling so proud!

Ice cubes chatter in nature's fridge,
Cracking jokes while we cross the ridge.
A polar bear wears a scarf too tight,
As penguins glide, what a silly sight!

Under the stars, we lay in the chill,
Sharing hot cocoa, what a thrill!
With marshmallow hats and smiles so wide,
We whisper secrets the snow can't hide!

The Silent Depths' Murmuring Lores

Beneath the crust where no one goes,
Fish tell tales of sneaky toes.
The seaweed giggles, what a gaff!
An octopus jokes, "Take a bath!"

Icicles dangle like wannabe stars,
Telling secrets of life behind bars.
Bubbles rise with a chuckle or two,
"Guess what, I just blew a shoe!"

Crabs do the cha-cha on an old wreck,
While sea horses laugh and stretch their neck.
The tides roll in, with their goofy sway,
"Let's dance a jig before we play!"

Beneath the waves, a concert in glee,
Mermaids sigh, "Please, just let us be!"
With singing shells and a bright coral hue,
Vows of laughter in the ocean blue!

Frozen Echoes of Yesteryears

In ancient frost where secrets slept,
Snowmen reminisce about ice they kept.
With carrot noses and eyes of coal,
Their tales of mischief make us whole!

Echoes laugh like a distant chime,
Remembering pranks from a frozen time.
"Remember the sledding that went awry?
I came in first, but they said I'd fly!"

Footprints lead to a snowball stash,
Concealed like treasure with a snowy splash.
A frozen thief steals a mitten or two,
As winter critters plot their next view!

Time freezes here in a playful way,
With clinking ice making fun today.
So let's toast with snowflakes, a drink of dew,
To memories bright, both old and new!

The Lullaby of the Icebound Realm

Crystalline stars above us glint,
While ice penguins frolic without a hint.
As snow spills laughter like fine confetti,
They slide down hills, oh so pretty!

Chilled whispers play on the frosty air,
"Wanna race?" a hare asks with flair.
Snowflakes tumble, swirling around,
Dancing a jig on this icy ground!

In the heart of winter, the stories fly,
Of seals on skateboards who pass by.
With every turn, giggles unfold,
As snow fort builders turn young and old!

So snuggle close, let the warmth ignite,
For laughter bonds us on this night.
In this realm, where the cool winds roam,
Together we weave our icy home!

Frosted Dreams of the Deep

In the depths where snickers float,
Frosty fish wear a winter coat.
They tell tales in bubbles so round,
Of snowmen built beneath the sound.

Crystals dance like sprites on ice,
Polar bears roll, oh, what a slice!
Snowflakes giggle in frosty glee,
As penguins waddle off to tea.

Beneath the surface, stuff gets wild,
Giggling seals act like it's a child.
They flip and flop with icy pride,
While whales sing jokes from the chilly tide.

The underwater world holds its cheer,
With frosted flakes sprinkled here.
So beneath the chill there's more in store,
Than just the quiet – it's laughter galore!

Secrets Enshrined in Winter's Grip

In a cabinet of frosty lore,
Snowflakes keep secrets to explore.
The squirrels plot with their fuzzy minds,
While frost-tinged laughter unwinds.

Penguins juggle ice cubes with care,
Dancing to rhythms found in the air.
The yeti hums a jolly tune,
While snowmen sip from cups made of rune.

Icicles spark like sharp little laughs,
Puffing out steam in their chilly baths.
Gossip flows like a river of slick,
As polar pups pull a prank, quick!

In a frozen world ripe with jest,
Chill laughter beats at every crest.
So lift a mug filled with snowy cheer,
The winter's grip is funny, oh dear!

Shadows Hidden by Winter's Blankets

Under the frost, shadows gleam bright,
Animals chuckle at winter's bite.
Hibernation? Nah, it's a fun snooze,
They dream of snacks and silly shoes.

The owls giggle in their snowy queue,
As snowflakes swirl, and giggles ensue.
Bears snort softly, belly in the snow,
While rabbits joke, 'We're all in the know!'

Hidden beneath a fluffy white cape,
Lies a penguin with a funny shape.
He waddles along with style so grand,
But trips over ice like it's all planned.

With laughter alive in a blanket of cold,
Frosted stories begin to unfold.
In the depths of winter, a chuckle ignites,
For behind the blank slate, glee always bites!

Lurking Echoes of the Chilled Night

Under the moon that giggles and grins,
A snowman pulls pranks with frosty fins.
To the echo of laughter, the night takes flight,
As icy whispers chortle with delight.

Creatures stumble in the snowy fluff,
'How many layers is really enough?'
Frogs in mittens leap like true pros,
As icy mist gives a sprinkle of woes.

Owls hoot jokes from their silver trees,
Chuckling softly with the chilly breeze.
Little squirrels toss snowballs wit' sass,
While ice sprites giggle, 'Don't you dare pass!'

In the frozen night, laughter does swell,
Echoes of joy, like a magic spell.
So tip your hat to the humor that glows,
For in this cold realm, chuckles overflow!

The Solitary Roar of the Frozen Abyss

In the depths where silence reigns,
A penguin slipped, it drives him insane.
He laughed and cried, a frosty dance,
While polar bears watched with mere glance.

The icebergs creaked with a goofy grin,
As seals played tag, they couldn't quite win.
One slipped and fell, a snowy surprise,
And the walruses chuckled, with wide-open eyes.

The snowy owls hooted a comical tune,
While frosty winds echoed a merry monsoon.
The iceberg's iceberg, tall and proud,
Cracked a joke that echoed loud.

In this frozen realm, joy takes its flight,
Where laughter abounds, in the pale moonlight.
Even in chill, the humor ignites,
In the roar of the deep, all smiles ignite.

Secrets of the Icy Womb

Beneath the crust of frozen glow,
A secret room where snowflakes grow.
A tiny hare hops with flair and luck,
Pretending to be a frosty duck.

A snowman winks, with a carrot nose,
Telling tales of the winter's prose.
While icicles dribbled, like ice cream fall,
Hilarity struck, the snowflakes call.

Squirrels dressed in a snowy cape,
Plotting pranks, their laughter can't escape.
They dress their tails in glittering gloss,
While the winter sun warns of frost.

In this chamber of chilly delight,
Where secrets are kept, day and night.
The humor flows like rivers of ice,
Creating laughter, oh so precise.

Murmurs of Snow and Ice

In a blizzard, where the snowflakes play,
A snowball fight brightens the gray.
The frost bites back, but who's in charge?
A dog rolls over and thinks he's large.

The igloos giggle as they start to melt,
Jokes on the ice, feelings heartfelt.
A beaver chews on his frozen bark,
While a fish swims by with a snarky remark.

Laughter echoes in the frozen air,
While snowmen brag without a care.
The frost is a stage for the silly and bright,
In a world where winter is pure delight.

From all around, the jests will arise,
With a winter dance that twirls and flies.
Join the fun in this snowy embrace,
And claim your giggle, and join the race.

The Enigma of the Frosted Whisper

Frosty thoughts float on the breeze,
With penguins chilling, aiming to please.
A walrus poses, striking a pose,
While seals surf the snow, and everyone rows.

A polar bear fumbles, a big snowball,
And the nearby snowflakes begin to fall.
They tickle his fur, he can't help but grin,
As laughter erupts amidst the din.

The frosty breeze carries jokes on its wake,
With each icy joke, a little heartache.
Icicles dangle, sporting their bling,
Making fun of snowflakes—what a wild fling!

In the frosted land, all dances align,
With secrets and humor, perfectly fine.
Embrace the chill, with hearts full of cheer,
For the tickles of frost bring laughter near.

Silent Echoes of Frost

In a snowman's hat, a squirrel quakes,
He thinks he's got the moves of Drake.
With frozen cheeks, he does a jig,
The laughter spreads, it's truly big.

A polar bear in shades so bright,
Sipping cocoa, what a sight!
He claims he's going on a spree,
But all he does is drink for free.

The icicles chime like tunes so sweet,
As skaters glide on frosty feet.
They slide and fall, the ice sings loud,
In this chill, we dance like a crowd.

The penguins waddle with a flair,
Stealing snacks without a care.
With frosty feet and rosy noses,
They throw a party, full of poses.

Secrets Caught in Glacial Breath

A snowflake lands with such a show,
It angers the wind, who yells, "Oh no!"
The flakes giggle, they start to race,
As frostbite gives that icy face.

A rabbit darts, his ears so tall,
Tip-toeing past a slippery sprawl.
He slips and tumbles, what a feat,
Yet grins and hops back on his feet.

In a chilly nook, the snowmen plot,
To start a snowball fight, why not?
They throw their fists, but miss the aim,
End up laughing, free from shame.

A frozen lake, with secrets deep,
Catches old fish; they wake from sleep.
"Did you hear the latest joke?" they ask,
As winter's chill becomes their task.

Murmurs from the Winter's Veil

The wind tickles trees, they start to sway,
With branches dancing, they seek to play.
Little birds chirp in muffled tone,
Cracking jokes from their frosty throne.

A snowshoe hare hops with a grin,
"Can you out-skip me?" "Oh, let's begin!"
They bounce and tumble on soft white,
Creating giggles 'neath pale moonlight.

A climbing cat in high gear runs,
Up to the roof for winter's fun.
He's caught slipping, his tail a blur,
Splat into snow, and what a spur!

The owls hoot secrets in the night,
Of winter pranks that give a fright.
The frost snaps back with all its might,
But laughter lingers, pure delight.

Beneath the Surface of Stillness

In icy realms where secrets play,
The frozen ground wishes to stay.
With feet on ice, the slip is slick,
Fishing tales turn to a slapstick.

A walrus slips, he tries to glide,
With flippers wide, he tries to ride.
He crashes down with a hearty thud,
While all the seals laugh in the mud.

A moose in boots struts through the trees,
He thinks he's cool, he's quite the tease.
With every stomp, the snowflakes swirl,
He twirls around, gives a big whirl.

Polar fillies on ice do prance,
In winter's ball, they take their chance.
A twinkle here, a frosty flip,
They giggle loud, make everyone trip.

Frostbitten Resilience

In a world so cold, yet full of cheer,
A penguin skids, but knows no fear.
He wears a scarf, a silly sight,
As snowflakes dance in pure delight.

With each slip and slide, he laughs it off,
His frosty buddies join in the scoff.
They build a snow fort, "We're the kings!"
Who knew ice could bring such funny things?

A polar bear sings, what a unique show,
In a tutu made from a blanket of snow.
He twirls and tumbles, a sight most rare,
As Arctic critters stop, pause, and stare.

A snowball fights while the seals cheer loud,
Frosty antics gather a giggling crowd.
As the sun sets low, with the day done right,
They wave goodnight to the frosty night.

Secrets of the Icebound Realm

In the land where frozen shadows play,
A walrus tells tales, come hear what he says.
His mustache twirls like a magical spell,
As laughter erupts from the snowy shell.

The fluffy white fox, with a wink and a grin,
Shares secrets of fish where the grumpy ones swim.
She dances on ice with her dainty paws,
While the creatures cheer, "Let's hear more applause!"

A seal with style, sporting shades at night,
Claims he can dance, in the moon's silver light.
But all he really does is flop and slide,
Yet all heartily laugh, not one tries to hide.

Underneath the stars, as stories unfold,
They feast on fish, chilled, but quite bold.
In this chill and frosty, yet joyful embrace,
Life's a big joke in this icy place.

Stories Whispered by the Frost

Oh, the tales of the chilly and bright,
A narwhal brags of his upturned might.
"I swept through storms, I conquered the waves!
My tusk's a sword, against icy knaves!"

A snowy owl gives a hoot and a wink,
"Tell me again, dear friends, what do you think?
Is it true the sun gives frostbite a rub?
Or that it once slept in a snowman's tub?"

Meanwhile, a goofy otter spins round,
In a whirl of laughter, he's lost and found.
"I slid on a glacier, oh what a ride!
But landed headfirst, with a snowball inside!"

Under the shimmering moon, they share bright dreams,
Mixing their giggles with sparkle and beams.
In this frosty playground, friendships ignite,
With each story told, the mood gets more bright.

Beneath the Crystal Canopy

Under the arches of crystal so grand,
A tiny mouse takes a brave stand.
With a hat made of snow, he struts through the cold,
Singing to seals as the legends unfold.

A snowman chortles, with a top hat so fine,
He claims he's a wizard, "Come, drink some brine!"
With snowballs a-flying, his magic's a hit,
Until he melts down, and whoops! He can't quit!

A fish in a scarf floats by with a grin,
He chuckles at seals who have forgotten to swim.
They blubber and splash, what a silly parade,
In this frozen realm, no joy is delayed!

At last, all together, they laugh in the night,
For friendships are timeless, and joy feels so right.
Beneath the canopy, in laughter and light,
Ice stories unfold, in delight's pure flight.

Milton Keynes UK
Ingram Content Group UK Ltd.
UKHW021242191124
451300UK00007B/195

9 789916 944905